Japan by Yacht

Japan by Yacht

A Voyage in the *Sunbeam*

Annie Brassey

TOYO PRess

First edition, 2019

Originally published as part of *A Voyage in the Sunbeam*

Published by TOYO PRess
Visit us at: **www.toyopress.com**

ISBN 978-94-92722-157

Arrival

Monday, January 29th, 1877

At four o'clock I was called to go on deck to see the burning mountain. The wind was still blowing hard, but we were among the islands, and in comparatively smooth water. The full moon still rode high in the heavens, her light being reflected in rainbow hues from the spray and foam that drifted along the surface of the water. On every side were islands and rocks, among which the sea boiled, and seethed, and swirled, while the roaring breakers dashed against the higher cliffs, casting great columns of spray into the air, and falling back in heavy rollers and surf.

Just before us rose Ō Island, with its cone-shaped volcano, 2,600 feet high, emitting volumes of smoke and flame. It was overhung by a cloud of white vapour, on the under side of which shone the lurid glare of the fires of the crater. Sometimes this cloud simply floated over the top of the mountain, from which it was quite detached; then there would be a fresh eruption; and after a few moments' quiet, great tongues of flame would shoot up and pierce through the overhanging cloud to the heavens above, while the molten lava rose like a fountain for a short distance, and then ran down the sides of the mountain.

It was wondrously beautiful. As a defence against the intense cold, we wrapped ourselves in furs, and stayed on deck watching the scene, until the sun rose glorious from the sea, and shone upon the snow-covered sides of Fuji-*yama*, called by the Japanese 'the matchless mountain.' It is an extinct crater, of the most perfect form, rising abruptly from a chain of very low mountains, so that it stands in unrivalled magnificence. This morning covered with the fresh-fallen snow, there was not a spot nor a fleck to be seen upon it, from top to bottom. It is said to be the youngest mountain in the world, the enormous mass having been thrown up in the course of a few days only 862 years B.C.

We reached the entrance to the Edo Bay about nine o'clock, and passed between its shores through hundreds of junks and fishing boats. I never saw anything like it before. The water was simply covered with them; and at a distance it looked as though it would be impossible to force a passage. As it was, we could not proceed very fast, so constantly were the orders to 'slow,' 'stop,' 'port,' 'starboard,' given; and I began at last to fear that it would be impossible to reach Yokohama without running down at least one boat.

The shores of the gulf, on each side, consist of sharp-cut little hills, covered with pines and cryptomerias, and dotted with temples and villages. Every detail of the scene exactly resembled the Japanese pictures one is accustomed to see in England; and it was easy to imagine that we were only gazing upon a slowly moving panorama, unrolling itself before us.

It was twelve o'clock before we found ourselves among the men-of-war and steamers lying near the port of Yokohama, and two o'clock before the anchor could be dropped.

During this interval we were surrounded by a swarm of boats, the occupants of which clamoured vociferously to be allowed on board, and in many cases they succeeded in evading the vigilance of the man at the gangway, by going round the other side and climbing over the rail. A second man was put on guard; but it was of no use, for we were invaded from all directions at once. We had a good many visitors also from the men-of-war, Japanese and English, and from the reporters of newspapers, full of curiosity, questions, and astonishment.

Having at last managed to get some lunch, Thomas [Brassey], went to bed to rest, after his two hard nights' work, and the rest of us went on shore. Directly we landed at the jetty we were rushed at by a crowd of *jinrikisha* men, each drawing a little vehicle not unlike a Hansom cab, without the seat for the driver—there being no horse to drive. The man runs between the shafts, and is often preceded by a leader, harnessed on in front, tandem fashion. Each of these vehicles holds one person, and they go along at a tremendous pace.

We went first to the consul's, where we got a few letters, and then to the post office, where many more awaited us. We had then to go to various places to order stores, fresh provisions, coals, and water, all of which were urgently needed on board, and to give directions for the repair of boats, spars, etc., with as little delay as possible. All this business, including the inevitable search for a good laundress, lay in the European quarter of the town, the appearance of which was not remarkable. But the people we met in the streets were a study in themselves. The children said they looked 'like fans walking about;' and it was not difficult to understand their meaning. The dress of the lower orders has remained precisely the same for hundreds of years; and before I had been ashore five minutes I realised more fully than I had ever done before the truthfulness of the representations of native artists, with which the fans, screens, and vases one sees in England are ornamented.

While we were going about, a letter was brought me, containing the sad news (received here by telegram) of the death of Thomas's mother. It was a terrible shock, coming, too, just as we were rejoicing in the good accounts from home which our letters contained. I went on board at once to break the bad news to Thomas. This sad intelligence realised a certain vague dread of something, we knew not what, which has seemed to haunt us both on our way hither.

Yokohama

Heavily plunged the breaking wave,
And foam flew up the lea,
Morning and evening the drifted snow
Fell into the dark grey sea.

When we awoke from our slumbers this morning, it was very cold and dark, and we heard strange noises. On going on deck to ascertain the cause of this state of things, we discovered that the sky-lights and portholes were all covered and blocked up with snow, and that the water froze as it came out of the hose, forming a sheet of ice on the deck. Masses of snow and ice were falling from the rigging, and everything indicated that our welcome to Japan would not be a warm one.

After breakfast we had many visitors, and received letters from Sir Harry and Lady Parkes, inviting us to go up to Edo tomorrow for a long day, to settle our future plans.

Having landed, we went with the consul to the native town, to see the curio shops, which are a speciality of the place. The inhabitants are wonderfully clever at making all sorts of curiosities, and the manufactories of so-called 'antique bronzes' and 'old china' are two of the most wonderful sights in Yokohama. The way in which they scrape, crack, chip, mend, and colour the various articles, cover them with dust, partially clean them, and imitate the marks and signatures of celebrated makers, is more creditable to their ingenuity than to their honesty. Still, there are a good many genuine old relics from the temples, and from the large houses of the reduced *daimyō*, to be picked up, if you go the right way to work, though the supply is limited. Dealers are plentiful, and travellers, especially from America, are increasing in numbers.

When we first made acquaintance with the shops we thought they seemed full of beautiful things, but even one day's shopping, in the company of experienced people, has educated our taste and taught us a great deal; though we have still much to learn. There are very respectable-looking lacquer cabinets ranging in price from 5 shillings. to 20 pounds. But they are only made for the foreign market. No such things exist in a Japanese home. A really good bit of old lacquer (the best is generally made into the form of a small box, a portable medicine-chest, or a chow-chow box) is worth from 20 pounds to 200 pounds. We saw one box, about three inches square, which was valued at 45 pounds, and a collection of really good lacquer would be costly and difficult to procure even here. The best specimens I have ever seen are at Lady Alcock's, but they are all either royal or princely presents, not to be bought with money.

The tests of good lacquer (*urushi*) are its exquisite finish, its satiny, oily feel, and the impossibility of making any impression on it with your thumb-nail. It is practically indestructible, and will wear for ever. All the poor as well as the rich people here use it, and have used it for centuries, instead of china and glass, for cups, saucers, dishes, bowls, which would need to be often washed in the hottest of water. It is said that the modern Japanese have lost the art of lacquer making. As an illustration I was told that many beautiful articles of lacquer, old and new, had been sent from this country to the Vienna Exhibition in 1873, but the price put on them was so exorbitant that few were sold, and nearly all had to be sent back to Japan. Just as the ship with these things on board reached the Edo Bay, she struck on a rock and sank in shallow water. A month or two ago a successful attempt was made to raise her, and to recover the cargo, when it was found that the new lacquer had been reduced to a state of pulp, while the old was not in the least damaged. I tell you the tale as it was told to me.

After a long day's shopping, we went to dine, in real Japanese fashion, at a Japanese teahouse. The establishment was kept by a very pleasant woman, who received us at the door, and who herself removed our exceedingly dirty boots before allowing us to step on to her clean mats. This was all very well, as far as it went; but she might as well have supplied us with some substitute for the objectionable articles, for it was a bitterly cold night, and the highly polished wood passages and steep staircase felt very cold to our shoeless feet.

The apartment we were shown into was so exact a type of a room in any Japanese house, that I may as well describe it once for all. The woodwork of the roof and the framework of the screens were all made of a handsome dark polished wood, not unlike walnut. The exterior walls under the verandah, as well as the partitions between the other rooms, were *shōji*, wooden latticework screens, covered with white paper, and sliding in grooves; so that you could walk in or out at any part of the wall you chose, and it was, in like manner, impossible to say whence the next comer would make his appearance. Doors and windows are, by this arrangement, rendered unnecessary, and do not exist. You open a little bit of your wall if you want to look out, and a bigger bit if you want to step out. The floor was covered with several thicknesses of very fine mats, each about six feet long by three broad, deliciously soft to walk upon. All mats in Japan are of the same size, and everything connected with house-building is measured by this standard. Once you have prepared your foundations and woodwork of the dimensions of so many mats, it is the easiest thing in the world to go to a shop and buy a house, ready made, which you can then set up and furnish in the scanty Japanese fashion in a couple of days.

On one side of the room was a slightly raised daïs, about four inches from the floor. This was the *tokonoma*. On it had been placed a stool, a little bronze ornament, and a china vase, with a branch of cherry-blossom and a few flag-leaves gracefully arranged. On the wall behind hung pictures, which are changed every month, according to the season of the year. There was no other furniture of any sort in the room. Four nice-looking Japanese girls brought us thick cotton quilts to sit upon, and braziers (*hibachi*) full of burning charcoal, to warm ourselves by. In the centre of the group another brazier was placed, protected by a square wooden grating, and over the whole they laid a large silk eiderdown quilt, to retain the heat. This is the way in which all the rooms, even bedrooms, are warmed in Japan, and the result is that fires are of very frequent occurrence. The brazier is kicked over by some restless or careless person, and in a moment the whole place is in a blaze.

Presently the eider down and brazier were removed, and our dinner was brought in. A little lacquer table, about six inches high, on which were arranged a pair of chopsticks, a basin of soup, a bowl for rice, a *sake* cup, and a basin of hot water, was placed before each person, whilst the four Japanese maidens sat in our midst, with fires to keep the *sake* hot, and to light the tiny pipes with which they were provided, and from which they wished us to take a whiff after each dish. *sake* is a sort of spirit, brewed from rice, always drunk hot, out of small cups. In this state it is not disagreeable, but we found it exceedingly nasty when cold.

Everything was well cooked and served, though the ingredients of some of the dishes, as will be seen from the following bill of fare, were rather strange to our ideas. Still they were all eatable, and most of them really palatable.

Soup.
Shrimps and Seaweed.
Prawns, Egg Omelette, and Preserved Grapes.
Fried Fish, Spinach, Young Rushes, and Young Ginger.
Raw Fish, Mustard and Cress, Horseradish, and Soy.
Thick Soup, of Eggs, Fish, Mushrooms, and Spinach; Grilled Fish.
Fried Chicken, and Bamboo Shoots.
Turnip Tops and Root Pickled.
Rice ad libitum in a large bowl.
Hot sake, Pipes and Tea.

The meal concluded with an enormous lacquer box of rice, from which all our bowls were filled, the rice being conveyed to our mouths by means of chopsticks. We managed very well with these substitutes for spoons and forks, the knack of using which, to a certain extent, is soon acquired. The long intervals between the dishes were beguiled with songs, music, and dancing, performed by professional singing and dancing girls. The music was somewhat harsh and monotonous; but the songs sounded harmonious, and the dancing was graceful, though it was rather posturing than dancing, great use being made of the fan and the long trailing skirts. The *geisha*, who were pretty, wore peculiar dresses to indicate their calling, and seemed of an entirely different stamp from the quiet, simply dressed waitresses whom we found so attentive to our wants. Still they all looked cheery, light-hearted, simple creatures, and appeared to enjoy immensely the little childish games they played amongst themselves between whiles.

After dinner we had some real Japanese tea, tasting exactly like a little hot water poured on very fragrant new-mown hay. Then, after a brief visit to the kitchen, which, though small, was beautifully clean, we received our boots, and were bowed out by our pleasant hostess and her attentive handmaidens.

On our return we had considerable difficulty in procuring a boat, our own boats being all ashore under repair. It was a beautiful moonlight night, but bitterly cold. The harbour being so full of shipping, our boatmen were at first puzzled how to find the yacht, till we pointed to the lights in the deck-house—always a good beacon at night in a crowded harbour.

Tokyo

Wednesday, January 31st

We left the yacht soon after eight o'clock, and started by the 9.34 a.m.
train for the city formerly called Edo, but latterly, since the emperor
has resided there, Tokyo, or eastern capital of Japan. The ground was
covered with snow, and there were several degrees of frost, but the
sun felt hot, and all the people were sunning themselves in the door-
ways or wide verandahs of their houses.

Yokohama has been so completely Europeanised, that it was not
until we had left it that we caught our first glimpse of Japanese life.
The whole landscape and the many villages looked very like a set of
living fans or tea-trays, though somehow the snow did not seem to
harmonise with it.

We crossed several rivers, and reached Tokyo in about an hour,
when we at once emerged into the midst of a clattering, chattering
crowd, amongst whom there did not seem to be a single European.
The reverberation, under the glass roof of the station, of the hundreds
of pairs of wooden clogs, pattering along, was something extraordinary. Giving up our tickets, and following the stream, we found ourselves surrounded by a still more animated scene, outside the station.
We were just deliberating what to do next, when a smart little Japanese, with a mailbag over his shoulder, stepped forward and said something about Sir Harry Parkes. He then popped us all into several
double and treble-manned *jinrikisha*, and started off himself ahead at

a tremendous pace, shouting and clearing the way for us. Tokyo is a genuinely Japanese town. Not a single foreigner resides within its limits, with the exception of the foreign ministers. There is no hotel nor any place of the kind to stay at; so that, unless you have friends at any of the legations, you must return to Yokohama the same day, which makes a visit rather a fatiguing affair. (I have since heard that there are two hotels at Tokyo, such as they are.)

Our first halting-place was the Zōjō-ji, the temple in Shiba Park, where most of the *shōgun* have been buried. It is a large enclosure, many acres in extent, in the centre of the city, with walls overgrown with creepers, and shadowed by evergreen trees, amid whose branches rooks caw, ravens croak, and pigeons coo, as undisturbedly as if in the midst of the deepest woodland solitude. I had no idea there was anything so beautiful in Japanese architecture as this temple. A primary idea in the architecture of Japan is evidently that of a tent among trees. The lines of the high, overhanging, richly decorated roofs, with pointed gable ends, are not straight, but delicately curved, like the suspended cloth of a tent. In the same way, the pillars have neither capital nor base, but seem to run through the building perpendicularly, without beginning or end. The principal temple was burnt down a few years ago; but there are many smaller ones remaining, built in exactly the same style, and all the tombs are perfect. Some people say the bodies are enclosed in coffins, filled with vermilion, but I need hardly say we had no opportunity of ascertaining the correctness of this statement. We entered several of the temples, which are perfect marvels of carving, gilding, painting, and lacquer work. Their style of decoration may be somewhat barbaric, but what a study they would form for an artist! Outside, where no colour is used, the overhanging roofs and the walls are carved with a depth and boldness, and yet a delicacy, I have seldom seen equalled; the doors and railings being of massive bronze, brought from Korea. Within, a dim religious light illumines and harmonises a dazzling mass of lacquer, gold, and painting. It is the grandest burial place imaginable; too good for the long line of men who have tyrannised over Japan and its lawful sovereigns for so many centuries past.

The streets of Tokyo were crowded with a motley throng up to the very gates of the citadel, where, within the first moat, stand all the *yashiki*, or residences of the *daimyō*. Each *yashiki* is surrounded by a blank wall, loopholed, and with a tower at each of the four corners. Within this outer wall is the court of the retainers, all of them 'two-sworded' men; then comes a second wall, also loopholed, inside which dwell distant relations of the *daimyō*; and then again a third enclosure, guarding the *daimyō* himself, with his immediate belongings. After crossing the third moat we reached the emperor's gardens and palace, the public offices, and the residences of the foreign ministers, all of which were formerly occupied by the *shōgun* and his ministers. On the waters of the inner moat were thousands of wild ducks and geese. Nobody is allowed to harm them, and the birds seem to be perfectly aware of this fact, for they disport themselves with the greatest confidence.

The English embassy is a nice red brick house, built in the centre of a garden, so as to be as secure as possible from fire or attack. After a most pleasant luncheon we looked over the nucleus of a second collection which Lady Parkes is beginning to form. Her former beautiful collection was burnt a few years ago, a most disheartening misfortune, especially as the opportunities for obtaining really old and good things in Japan are diminishing day by day.

A little later we started in great force, some in carriages and some on horseback, attended by running grooms, to see something more of the city. These men think nothing of running by the side of a horse and carriage some forty miles a day. They form a distinct class, and when working on their own account wear little clothing. When in the service of private individuals they are dressed in tight-fitting dark-blue garments, with short capes, fastened to their arms, and large hats.

Just outside the embassy we passed two of the finest of the still existing *yashiki*, the larger one being used as the Home Office, the other as the Foreign Office.

There is always a festival going on in some part of Tokyo. Today there had been a great wrestling-match, and we met all the people coming away. Such crowds of *jinrikisha*, full of gaily dressed and painted women and children, with their hair plastered into all sorts of inconceivable shapes, and decorated with artificial flowers and glittering pins! We met six of the wrestlers themselves, riding in *jinrikisha*—big men, prodigiously fat, and not at all, according to our ideas, in fighting or wrestling condition. One of their *jinrikisha* men stumbled and fell, just as they passed us, and the wrestler shot out, head over heels, and lay, a helpless ball of fat, in the middle of the road, till somebody came and picked him up. He was not in the least hurt, and, as soon as he was set on his feet again, began to belabour the poor *jinrikisha* man most unmercifully. After a long and delightful drive we arrived at the station just in time to catch the train.

The return journey to Yokohama, in the omnibus-like railway carriages, was very cold, and the *jinrikisha* drive to the Grand Hotel colder still. But a roaring fire and a capital dinner soon warmed and comforted us.

After dinner we looked over a fine collection of photographs of Japanese scenery and costumes, and then returned to the *Sunbeam* in the house boat belonging to the hotel, which was prettily decorated with bright-coloured lanterns, and which afforded welcome shelter from the biting wind.

Enoshima

Careful arrangements have been made for our excursion to the Island of Enoshima, and to see the great Buddha figure of Daibutsu at Kamakura. By eight o'clock we had landed, and packed ourselves into a funny little shaky carriage, drawn by four horses. We drove quickly through the town, past the station, along the Tōkaidō, or imperial road, running from Tokyo to Kyoto, and on which so many foreigners have been murdered even within the last ten years. Now, however, it is perfectly safe.

The houses are one story high, and their walls are made of the screens I have already described. These screens were all thrown back, to admit the morning air, cold as it was. We could consequently see all that was going on within, in the sitting room in front, and even in the bedrooms and kitchen. At the back of the house there was invariably a little garden to be seen, with a miniature rockery, a tree, and a lake; possibly also a bridge and a temple. Even in the gardens of the poorest houses an attempt at something of the sort had been made. The domestic occupations of the inhabitants being conducted in this public manner, a very good idea might be obtained, even at the end of a few miles' drive, of how the lower class of Japanese wash and dress themselves and their children, how very elaborate the process of hair-dressing is, to say nothing of a bird's-eye view of the ground-plan of the houses, the method of cooking food, etc.

As we emerged into the open country the landscape became very pretty, and the numerous villages, nestling in the valleys at the foot of the various small hills, had a most picturesque appearance. At a stone quarry that we passed, on the side of a mountain, there were about seventy men at work, without any clothing, though the thermometer was far below freezing point. The Japanese are a sensitive nation, and finding that foreigners were astonished and shocked at the habits of the people, in going about without clothes, and in bathing in public and at their house doors, they passed a law prohibiting these customs in towns. In the country the more primitive customs are still in force, and every dwelling has its half-open bathhouse, whilst the people do as they like in the matter of clothing.

After stopping twice on the road, to drink the inevitable tea, we changed from our carriage to *jinrikisha*, each drawn and pushed by four strong men, bowling along at a merry pace. The sun was very warm in the sheltered valleys, and the abundance of evergreens of all kinds quite deluded one into the belief that it was summer time, especially as camellias grew like forest trees, covered with red and white bloom, amidst a dense tangle of bamboos and half-hardy palms. There were many strange things upside down to be seen on either hand— horses and cows with bells on their tails instead of on their necks, the quadrupeds well clothed, their masters without a scrap of covering, tailors sewing from them instead of to them, a carpenter reversing the action of his saw and plane. It looked just as if they had originally learned the various processes in 'Alice's Looking-glass World' in some former stage of their existence.

We had not long left the town before our men began to undress each other, for their clothes were so tight that it required no inconsiderable effort to remove them. Some of them were beautifully tattooed. My wheeler had the root of a tree depicted on one foot, from which sprang the trunk and branches, spreading gradually, until on his back and chest they bore fruit and flowers, amongst which birds were perched. On his other leg was a large stork, supposed, I imagine, to be standing under the shadow of the same tree. Another man had human figures tattooed all over him, in various attitudes.

In less than an hour we reached the narrow strip of land that at low water connects the island or peninsula of Enoshima with the mainland. This isthmus was covered with natives gathering shells and seaweed, casting their nets, and pushing off or dragging up their boats; whilst an island rose fresh and green from the sea, with a background of snowy mountains, stretching across the bay, above which Fujiyama towered grandly. This name signifies 'not two, but one mountain,' the Japanese thinking it impossible that there can be another like it in the world. The lovely little island is called Enoshima, and is conical in shape and covered with evergreens and Buddhist temples, with a few small fishing villages scattered on its shores. We walked right across it in about an hour, so you may imagine it is not very large. The sea teems with curiously shaped fish and beautiful shells. The staple food of the inhabitants seems to be those lovely 'Venus's ears,' (Haliotis) as they are called—a flattish univalve, about as big as your hand, with a row of holes along the edge, and a lining of brilliant black mother-of-pearl. These were lying about in heaps mixed with white mother-of-pearl shells, as big as your two fists, and shaped like a snail shell.

Our *jinrikisha* men deposited us at the bottom of the main street of the principal village, to enter which we passed through a simple square arch of a temple. The street was steep and dirty, and consisted principally of shellfish and seaweed shops.

An old priest took us in hand, and, providing us with stout sticks, marched us up to the top of the hill to see various temples, and splendid views in many directions. The camellias and evergreens on the hillside made a lovely framework for each little picture, as we turned and twisted along the narrow path. I know not how many steps on the other side of the island had to be descended before the sea beach was reached. Here is the Iwaya Cave, stretching five hundred feet straight below high-water mark, with a shrine to Benten-*sama*, the Lucina of Japan. Having been provided with candles, we proceeded a few hundred feet through another cave, running at right angles to the first.

As it would have been a long steep walk back, and I was very tired, we called to one of the numerous fishing boats near the shore, and were quickly conveyed round to our original starting place. Before we said goodbye, one of the old priests implored to be allowed to dive into the water for half a dollar. His request was complied with, and he caught the coin most successfully.

We lunched at a teahouse, our meal consisting of fish of all kinds, deliciously cooked, and served, fresh from the fire, in a style worthy of Greenwich; and as we had taken the precaution to bring some bread and wine with us, we were independent of the usual rice and *sake*.

Kamakura

We next proceeded on our way towards the Daibutsu, or Great Buddha, situated within the limits of what was once the large city of Kamakura, now only a collection of small hamlets. As all Japanese cities are built of wood, it is not wonderful that they should in time entirely disappear, and leave no trace behind them. But there still remain some of the columns of the temple which once existed in the gardens surrounding the idol. Now he is quite alone, and for centuries has this grand old figure sat, exposed to the elements, serenely smiling on the varying scene beneath him. The figure is of bronze, and is supposed to have been cast about the year 1250 or 1260.

It is some fifty feet high, with golden eyes and a silver spiral horn on the forehead. It is possible to sit or stand on the thumb, and within the hollow body an altar is erected, at which the priests officiate. Sitting there, amidst a grove of enormous cryptomerias and bamboos, there is an air of ineffable silent strength about that solitary figure, which affords a clue to the tenacity with which the poorer classes cling to Buddhism. The very calmness of these figures must be more suggestive of relief and repose to the poor weary worshippers than the glitter of the mirror and crystal ball to be found in the Shintō temples. The mirror is intended to remind believers that the Supreme Being can see their innermost thoughts as clearly as they can perceive their own reflection; while the crystal ball is an emblem of purity. Great store is set by the latter, especially if of large size and without flaw; but to my mind the imperfect ones are the best, as they refract the light and do not look so much like glass.

Close by—also part of Kamakura—there is the Tsurugaoka Hachiman-gu, a fine temple dedicated to the god of war. But we were pressed for time, and hurried back to the little carriages. The homeward drive was long and cold. But the Tōkaidō looked very pretty lighted up, the shadows of the inmates being plainly visible on the paper walls, reminding one of a scene in a pantomime. On our way down a very steep hill we met the men carrying a *kago*. It is a most uncomfortable-looking basket-work contrivance, in which it is impossible to sit or lie with ease. These *kago* used formerly to be the ordinary conveyance of Japan but are now replaced by the *jinrikisha* and seldom met with, except in the mountains or in out-of-the-way places.

The Market

Friday, February 2nd

I was called at five o'clock, and at half-past six Mabelle and I started for the market. It was blowing a gale, and our four oarsmen found it as much as they could do to reach the shore. The Shanghai mailboat was just in, and I pitied the poor passengers, who were in all the misery of being turned out into the cold of the early morning, with the spray breaking over them as they sat in the small boats.

The market at Yokohama is one of the sights of the place. There were large quantities of birds and game of all kinds—pheasants with tails six feet long, of a rare copper-coloured variety, ducks, pigeons, small birds, hares, deer, rabbits. The fish market was well supplied, especially with cuttlefish. They are not inviting-looking, but are considered a delicacy here. A real octopus, in a basket, with its hideous body in the centre, and its eight arms, covered with suckers, arranged in the form of a star, is worth from a dollar to a dollar and a half, according to its size. I was not tempted to make any purchases.

From the market we went to one or two small shops in back streets, and from there over the bluffs, in the teeth of a bitterly cold wind, to a nursery garden, to examine the results of *bonsai*, the Japanese art of dwarfing and distorting trees. Some specimens were very curious and some beautiful, but most were simply hideous. We saw tiny old gnarled fruit trees, covered with blossom, and Scotch firs and other forest trees, eight inches high, besides diminutive ferns and creepers.

It being now half-past nine o'clock, we went to the hotel to meet the rest of the party for breakfast, and at one o'clock we returned to the *Sunbeam*. At half-past one Lady Parkes and several other friends from Tokyo came on board to luncheon. They told of three disastrous fires that had taken place in Tokyo yesterday, by which the Home Office—one of the finest old *yashiki*—and several smaller edifices had been destroyed.

After the departure of our guests we paid another visit to the shore, and saw the foxhounds. They are a nice pack, and have good kennels outside the foreign settlement. They were out this morning at 6.30, but unfortunately we did not know of it. There are plenty of foxes, and some very fair country not far from here; so they expect to have good sport.

We weighed anchor at 8.30 p.m. and proceeded under steam. At 11.30, when off Tsurugi-saki, we set some of the head canvas. It was a cold night, with sleet and snow, though it was not blowing as hard as during the day.

Kobe

Manners with fortunes, humours change with climes,
Tenets with books, and principles with times.

Saturday, February 3rd
The occasional glimpses of the coast scenery through the sleet and snow were very fine. We passed Ōshima and Kojima Islands and the Shima Peninsula. But Mabelle [Brassey] and I spent most of the day in bed; she suffering from a blow from the boom, which had produced slight concussion of the brain, and I having a wretched cold, which has been gradually getting worse the last few days, and which has quite taken away my voice.

Sunday, February 4th
It was blowing hard all day, raining, snowing, and sleeting. The scenery appeared to be pretty, and we passed through crowds of picturesque junks.

At 4.25 we rounded Tomoga-shima, and at 9 p.m. anchored off the town of Kobe, or Hyōgo.

These constant changes of names are very puzzling. Miako and Edo, which we did know something about, are quite cut out, and replaced by Kyoto and Tokyo. Oddly enough, the same syllables, reversed, mean 'capital of the western empire' and 'capital of the eastern empire' respectively.

Monday, February 5th

By seven o'clock a boat was alongside with letters from the consul and Sir Harry Parkes, who had kindly made all the necessary arrangements for us to see the opening of the railway from Kobe to Kyoto, and for the presentation of the gentlemen to the emperor.

It certainly was a great opportunity for seeing a Japanese holiday crowd, all dressed in their best. Thousands and thousands of people were in the streets, who, though naturally anxious to see as much as possible, behaved in the most quiet and orderly manner. The station was beautifully decorated with evergreens, camellias, and red berries. Outside there was a most marvellous pavilion, the woodwork of which had been entirely covered with evergreens, and ornamented with life-size dragons and phoenixes (the imperial insignia of Japan), all made in flowers. The roof was studded with large chrysanthemums—the private device of the emperor, that of the *shōgun* being three hollyhock leaves. The sides of the pavilion were quite open, the roof being simply supported on pillars; so that we could see everything that went on, both inside and out. The floor was covered with red cloth; the daïs with an extremely ugly Brussels carpet, with a large pattern. On this the emperor's throne was placed, with a second canopy above it.

Thomas in R.N.R. uniform, the other gentlemen in evening dress, accompanied the consul on to the platform to receive the emperor; while the children and I went with Mrs. Annesley to seats reserved for the foreign representatives. There were not many Europeans present; but the platform was densely crowded with Japanese, sitting on their heels, and patiently waiting to see the extraordinary sight of their hitherto invisible spiritual Emperor brought to them by a steam engine on an iron road.

The men had all had their heads fresh shaven, and their funny little pigtails rearranged for the occasion. The women's hair was elaborately and stiffly done up with light tortoiseshell combs and a large pin, and decorated with artificial flowers. Some of the children were gaily dressed in red and gold under garments, the prevailing colour of the costumes being dark blue, turned up with red. They also wore gay embroidered *obi*, or large sashes, which are put on in a peculiar fashion. They are of great width, and are fastened tightly round the waist, while an enormous bow behind reaches from between the shoulders to far below the hips. The garments fit tightly in front, while at the back they form a sort of huge bunch. On their high-heeled clogs the women walk with precisely the same gait as ladies in high-heeled boots. In fact, so exactly do the Japanese women (you never see Japanese *ladies* walking about in the streets) caricature the present fashionable style of dress in Europe, that I have formed a theory of my own on the subject, and this is it.

Some three or four years ago, among other proposed reforms in Japan, the ministers wished the empress and her court to be dressed in European fashion. Accordingly a French milliner and dressmaker, with her assistants, was sent for from Paris, and in due time arrived. The Empress and her ladies, however, would not change their style of dress. They knew better what suited them, and in my opinion they were very sensible. This is what I hear. Now what I think is, that the Parisienne, being of an enterprising turn of mind, thought that she would not take so long a journey for nothing—that if the Japanese ladies would not follow European fashions, at least European ladies should adopt the Japanese style. On her return to Paris I am convinced that she promulgated this idea, and gradually gave it effect. Hence the fashions of the last two years.

Watching the crowd occupied the time in a most interesting manner, till the firing of guns and the playing of bands announced the arrival of the imperial train. The emperor was received on the platform, and after a very short delay he headed the procession along the covered way on to the daïs.

He is a young, not very good-looking man, with rather a sullen expression, and legs that look as though they did not belong to him—I suppose from using them so little, and sitting so much on his heels; for until the last few years the emperor has always been considered far too sacred a being to be allowed to set foot on the earth. He was followed by his highest minister, the foreign ministers, and a crowd of Japanese dignitaries, all, with one or two exceptions, in European official dress, glittering with gold lace. I believe it was the first time that many of them had ever worn it. At any rate, they certainly had never learned to put it on properly. It would have driven to distraction the tailor who made them, to see tight-fitting uniforms either left un-buttoned altogether, or hooked askew from top to bottom, and to be-hold the trousers turned up and disfigured by the projecting tags of immense side-spring boots, generally put on the wrong feet. Some of the visitors had no gloves, while others wore them with fingers at least three inches too long. Certainly a court dresser as well as a court tailor ought to be appointed to the emperor's establishment, before the European costume becomes generally adopted.

I could not help thinking that the two or three old conservative ministers who had stuck to their native dress must have congratu-lated themselves on their firmness, when they saw the effect of the unaccustomed garments upon their *confrères*. The old court dress of the *daimyō* is very handsome, consisting of rich silks and brocades, with enormously long loose trousers trailing two or three feet on the ground, and with sleeves, like butterfly wings, of corresponding di-mensions. A small high-peaked black cap is worn on the head, to ac-commodate the curious little cut-off pigtail, set up like a cock's comb, which appears to be one of the insignia of a *daimyō*'s rank in Japan.

As soon as the people had arranged themselves into three sides of a square, Sir Harry Parkes read an address, and presented his five compatriots to the emperor, who replied in inaudible but no doubt suitable terms. Then the governor of Kobe had to read an address, and I pitied the poor man from the bottom of my heart. His knees shook, his hands trembled, and his whole body vibrated to such an extent, that his cocked hat fell and rolled on the floor of the daïs, and finally hopped down the steps, while the address nearly followed its example. How thankful he must have felt when it was over! .

The proceedings in the pavilion being now at an end, the emperor walked down the middle of the assembly, followed by all his ministers in single file, on his way to the luncheon tent. After they had gone, we inspected the imperial railway carriage, the soldiers, guns, etc., and just as we were leaving the station yard, to look at the daylight fireworks they were letting off in honour of the occasion, a salute announced the departure of the emperor for Kyoto.

We lunched at the consulate, our gentlemen changed to more comfortable attire, and then we went to see a Buddhist temple, supposed to be rather a fine specimen of woodwork. It is specially curious on account of some monkeys and a white horse, each kept in a sort of side shrine. Every worshipper at the temple stopped before these shrines, and for a small coin bought rice or beans to feed them with, through the priest. Whether it was an act of worship, or simply of kindness, I could not discover, though I paid several visits to the spot during our stay at Kobe.

From the temple we went to the shops in the main street of Hyōgo, and full of interest and temptation we found them. The town itself is quite Japanese, and consists, as usual, of wooden houses, narrow streets, and quaint shops. Today all was *en fête*, in preparation for the illuminations tonight.

Kobe, the foreign settlement, is, on the contrary, brandnew, spick and span, with a handsome parade, and grass and trees, planted boulevard fashion, along the edge of the sea. It is all remarkably clean, but quite uninteresting. Tonight, however, it looked very well, illuminated by thousands and thousands of coloured paper lanterns, arranged in all sorts of fanciful devices. It was dark and clear, and there was no wind, so that everything went off well.

Kyoto

Tuesday, February 6th

My cold being still bad, Mabelle by no means well yet, and Thomas very busy, we at first thought of keeping quiet today. But our time is so short, that we could not afford to waste it; so half our party started early for Kyoto, it being arranged that Thomas and Mabelle should follow us by an early train tomorrow. It was a wet cheerless day, and the country did not look its best. Still, the novelty of the scenes around could not fail to make them interesting. The Japanese have an intense horror of rain, and it was ludicrous to see the peasants walking along with scarcely any clothes on except a pair of high clogs, a large hat, and a paper umbrella. We crossed several large bridges, stopped at a great many stations, where heaps of native travellers got in and out, and finally reached Kyoto at half-past two o'clock. It was still raining, and all the *jinrikisha* men wore their large rain hats and rain cloaks, made either of reeds or of oiled paper. Most of the *jinrikisha*, too, had oiled paper hoods and aprons.

The drive to our hotel, through long, narrow, crowded, picturesque streets, seemed long and wearisome. It was still a holiday, and remains of the previous night's illuminations were to be seen on all sides. The large paper lanterns still remained fastened to the high poles, with an open umbrella at the top to afford protection from the rain.

Kyoto is a thoroughly Japanese town. I do not suppose it contains a single European resident, so that the manners and customs of the natives may be seen in perfection. Its theatres and jugglers are famous throughout Japan. In the suburb, where the two hotels are situated, stand numberless teahouses and other places of entertainment. Our hotel is situated halfway up the hill called Maruyama.

After about three-quarters of an hour's ride in the *jinrikisha*, we were deposited at the bottom of a flight of steps, which appeared to lead to a temple, but by which we reached the hotel in about five minutes. We were received by servants, who bowed to the ground, but did not speak a word which we could understand. The rooms looked clean and comfortable, and the dining room boasted a table and six chairs, besides several screens and *hibachi*. The bedrooms, too, had beds, screens, and washstands; quite an unexpected luxury. Still more so was a strip of glass about halfway up the screens, through which we could admire the fine prospect. Anything in the shape of a transparent window is a complete novelty in a Japanese house, where, in winter, you feel as if you were imprisoned. The view from the verandah of the hotel over the pretty fantastic garden, the temple grounds, the town of Kyoto, and the mountains in the distance was an endless source of delight to me.

The servants soon produced a luncheon, excellently well cooked, and directly we had finished it we sallied forth again to see what we could before dark. First we went to the temple of Gion, a fine building, standing in extensive grounds, and surrounded by smaller temples and houses for the priests. The Dutch envoys used to stay here when they were brought through the country, like prisoners, to pay their annual tribute for being allowed to trade with Japan. They were subjected to all kinds of indignities, and used to be made to dance and sing, pretend to be drunk, and play all sorts of pranks, for the amusement of the whole court as well as for the emperor and the empress, hidden behind a grating.

From Gion we went to see other temples, and wandered about under the large conifers of all kinds, trying to find out the quarters of the British Legation for some time, until Sir Harry Parkes returned. The rooms at his residence were comfortable, but cold-looking, for mats and paper screens do not look nice in a frost. There were tables and chairs and paraffin lamps, but no bedsteads, only about a dozen cotton and silk quilts, some of which were supposed to serve as a couch, while others were to be used as coverings.

Sir Harry has had, I fear, a great deal of trouble about the *Sunbeam*. She is the first vessel of the kind ever seen in Japan, with the exception of the one sent out in 1858 as a present from the Queen to the then *shōgun*, and now used by the emperor. The officials, it seems, cannot make the *Sunbeam* out. 'Is she a man-of-war? We know what that is.' 'No.' 'Is she a merchant ship?' 'No, she is a yacht.' But what can be the object of a vessel without guns is quite beyond their comprehension. At last it has been settled that, in order to be like other nations, the Japanese officials will not force us to enter at the Custom House, or to pay a fine of sixty dollars a day for not doing so. As a matter of precedent, it was important that the point should be settled, though I hardly imagine that many yachts will follow our example, and come out to Japan through the Straits of Magellan and across the Pacific.

As it was now growing late, we returned to the hotel for dinner. The night was cold, and *hibachi* and lamps alike failed to warm the thinly walled and paper-screened room.

Sir Harry Parkes came and spent the evening with us, and taught us more about Japan in two or three hours than we could have learned by much study of many books. The fact is, that in this fast-changing country guidebooks get out of date in two or three years. Besides which, Sir Harry has been one of the chief actors in many of the most prominent events we have recently been reading about. To hear him describe graphically the wars of 1868, and the Christian persecutions in 1870, with the causes that led to the revolution, and the effect it has had on the country, was indeed interesting. Still more so was his account of his journey hither to force the newly emerged emperor and his ministers to sign the treaty, which had already received the assent (of course valueless) of the deposed *shōgun*.

Wednesday, February 7th
A misty but much warmer morning succeeded a wet night. At 8.30 Sir Harry Parkes and two other gentlemen arrived, and we all started at

once in *jinrikisha* to see what could be seen in the limited time at our disposal.

We went first to the Sōkuku-ji, the temple described elaborately in books by other travellers. It is specially interesting to Europeans, as it was the temple assigned to the foreign envoys when they paid their first visit to the emperor in 1868. Sir Harry Parkes showed us all their apartments, and the large though subsidiary temple once used as a hospital, and we afterwards went to see the service performed in the temple. A dozen bonzes, or priests, were sitting round in a circle, chanting monotonously from ponderous volumes, with an occasional accompaniment from a gong or drum. Incense was being burned, vestments worn, processions formed, and prayers offered to Buddha to intercede with the Supreme Being. The accessories and surroundings were of course different, but the ceremonial struck me as being much the same as that in use at Roman Catholic places of worship. Mr. Simpson, however, thinks differently. He says:

I was only a month in Japan, and that is far too short a time for anything like serious study; but I was much struck by the temples, and I find I have some notes in my book comparing them with the Jewish. How any direct connection could possibly exist, is far beyond my powers of conjecture; but I will state the points of resemblance, and leave others to inquire further and collect additional information.

Wood and bronze to this day furnish the material of which temples are constructed in Japan, with stone as a base. Such also were the materials of Solomon's temple. There are enclosures round each court or shrine, and sometimes these courts are three in number. Hills or groves are usually sites for a temple, the ascent to which is by a long flight of steps; usually two flights give access to the shrine. One is long, straight, and steep, for the men; the other, less steep, but curved, is for the women. It will be remembered that it was the great stairs at Solomon's temple that so impressed the Queen of Sheba. Small shrines or miniature temples, called Tennō-sama, or

"Heaven's Lord," are carried on staves, like the Ark of the Covenant, at their religious ceremonies.

The inner shrine, or Holy of Holies, is small, and a cube, or nearly so, in proportion. It is usually detached behind the other portions of the temple, the door being closed, so that it cannot be seen into, and it generally contains, not an image, but a tablet, or what the Japanese call a *gohei*, or piece of paper, cut so that it hangs down in folds on each side. In the early days of writing, a tablet was a book, a stylus the pen. The stone on which the law was inscribed was only a form of the book, and the Chinese ancestral tablet, or other tablet, in a temple, is only a variety of this book form. These *gohei* are so common in Japan, and occupy so important a place in all their temples, that I had a great desire to know what they originally meant; but as on many questions of this kind I could get no information, the only suggestion that presented itself to me was, that it might be some form of the book, for the book was a very sacred thing in past time, and that which is yet called the "Ark," in a Jewish synagogue, contains now nothing but a book.

There is a distinct priesthood who wear vestments, and they use incense, music, and bells. There are two religions in Japan, Buddhism and Shintōism; the latter being the primitive faith, and the former an importation from China. The forms of the two have become slightly mixed, both in the construction of their temples and in the ceremonial; but the remarks I have just made apply particularly to the Shintō religion.

One of the late acts of the government has been to declare the Shintō, as the old religion of the country, to be the only state faith. This is the disestablishment of Buddhism, but it does not imply its suppression. The Buddhist priests complain very much, saying that their temples are not now so popular, and many are being closed. Speculators are buying up their fine bronze bells, and sending them home to be coined into English pennies and halfpennies. Changes in faith present many strange aspects, and this is certainly a curious one.

We strolled about the temple grounds, and ascended the hill to see the famous bell, which is the second biggest in Japan. The immense beam that strikes it was unlashed from the platform for our edification, and the bell sent forth a magnificent sound, pealing over the city and through the woods. At one of the gates there is a curious staircase, leading up to the top, and there, over the gate, is seated a figure of Buddha, surrounded by twelve disciples, all carved in wood and coloured. They are quite worth a scramble up to see.

From the Sōkuku-ji we went right across the city to the temple of Nishi Hongan-ji. On our way we were more than once stopped and turned off the direct road, which was kept by soldiers for the passage of the emperor to worship at the tombstone of his innumerable ancestors, real or imaginary. Being a spiritual Emperor, he has to be well kept up to his religious duties, and is always being sent off to worship at some shrine or another, in order to maintain his popularity with the people, his ministers meanwhile managing the affairs of state. Sanjô Sanetomi and Iwakura Tomomi went off in haste today to Tokyo, as there are rumours of a rebellion in the south.

The Nishi Hongan-ji is one of the largest and finest temples we have yet seen, even in spite of a large portion having been destroyed by the disastrous fire of 1864. The gates are splendidly ornamented, with carved chrysanthemum flowers. The centre temple is very fine, and is surrounded by smaller rooms, all decorated by the best Japanese artists of about two hundred years ago. Notice had been sent that the English minister was coming with a party of friends, and everything had accordingly been prepared for our reception. In some places they had even put down carpets, to obviate the necessity of our having to take off our boots. The Abbot was out, which I much regretted, for he belongs to the Jōdo Shinshū, a sect of Buddhism, and has more than once remarked to English visitors that he thought their own principles were so enlightened that they were paving the way for a higher form of religion, in the shape of Christianity—rather a startling confession to come from the lips of a Buddhist priest.

After spending a long time among the paintings, wood carvings, lacquers, bronzes, and gardens, we left the temple, and crossed several courtyards, before the main street was reached. Then, after a short walk, we came to another beautiful garden, laid out like a miniature park, with lakes, bridges, rocks, streams, canals, and pavilions. All these surround the Jurakudai, built by the celebrated *shōgun*, Taikō-*sama*, in the fifteenth century. Here, again, everything was prepared for our reception. Fires were lighted, flowers arranged, carpets laid down, and fruit and cakes placed in readiness, with *hibachi* to warm each and all of us. We went all over the house, which differs little from a Japanese house of the present day, except that a higher style of art was employed in its construction and decoration.

From here we went to quite another quarter of the city to see Nijō castle, formerly the *shōgun*'s palace, now used as a sort of police office. It is built on the same plan of three enclosures as all the *yashiki*, though on a very different scale from the one at Tokyo. There, the *shōgun* reigns in undisturbed sovereignty. Here, he appears as a humble servant of his rightful master—really his prisoner. The late *shōgun*, after the last battle, fought at this place, fled to his castle at Osaka, where, though he might have held out for an indefinite period, he preferred to surrender. Two of his ministers came to him and represented that he must not only think of himself, but of the party who supported the Shogunate, and that as he had betrayed them by false hopes he had no choice but to perform *harakiri*. This he refused to do, although they set him the example; and he is now living as a private individual on an estate in the country, not far from Tokyo, where he amuses himself with hunting, shooting, and fishing. It is said that it is possible he may one day join the ministry of the present emperor.

From the *shōgun*'s palace we drove to the Kyoto Gyoen, or court quarter of the town, where the emperor and all his relatives live, in palaces, surrounded by large gardens, enclosed in whitewashed walls. We saw the whole of Taikō-*sama*'s household furniture and wearing apparel, the celebrated swords of Yoritomo, called the 'knee-cutter' and the 'beard-cutter,' from their wonderful sharpness, and many other interesting objects.

Here we said goodbye to Sir Harry Parkes, and returned across the town by another route to our hotel to lunch, after which we made another expedition to one or two more temples, and then to a pawnbroker's shop, in the heart of the city, which had been strongly recommended to us. The exterior did not look promising; the shop itself was small and dirty; and they had to take some very filthy garments out of the way before we could enter. Once inside it was a very different story. They showed us splendid old embroideries, and quantities of second-hand court dresses, embroidered in gold, silver, and colours, with exquisite designs. The empress has thirteen ladies of honour, who wear their best dresses only twice, and then sell them: hence the pawnbrokers abundant stock.

Wherever we went a large but perfectly civil crowd followed us, and people ran on before to tell others to come to their doors and look at us, though we were under the charge of an officer and two men. It was now getting dark, and we were very tired, so we at last turned back, and once more climbed those weary steps to our hotel. Tonight there is some *fête* going on in this suburb, and the whole place is alive with lights, dancing, music, and tum-tums.

After dinner all our purchases arrived, each accompanied by at least four or five men. Other people had heard of our visit, and had brought more things for us to look at, so that the room soon resembled a bazaar. At last we got rid of them, having settled that they should pack our things and take them down to Kobe, where they would be paid for. The Japanese shopkeepers, though difficult to deal with, are incorruptible once the bargain is made. They pack most carefully, frequently adding boxes, bags, and baskets, not originally included in the purchase, in order that the articles may travel more safely. The smallest article is sure to be put in, and the greatest care is taken of everything, even if they know you do not mean to open the cases for months.

If it were only warmer, how delightful it would all be! The cold spoils everything to a certain extent. At night we have to choose whether to be half frozen in our beds, or stifled with the fumes of charcoal from the *hibachi*.

Thursday, February 8th

The sunrise over the city, with the river and mountains beyond, was superb. We breakfasted at eight; but even by that hour the courtyard and passage were crowded with vendors of curiosities of all sorts, and no doubt great bargains might have been picked up. But we had no time to lose, for our train started at 9.30, and we had a delightfully rapid drive to the station through the sunny streets of Kyoto.

Arrived at Kobe, we went first to lunch with some friends, and immediately after hastened on board to receive the foreign ministers and other friends, and did not land again that evening.

Osaka

We left by ten o'clock train for Osaka, which has been called the Venice of Japan. It is intersected by innumerable rivers and canals, and boats were continually making their appearance at points where they were least expected, as our *jinrikisha* men hurried us along the narrow and not very sweet-smelling streets. We went so fast that, more than once before we reached the Mint, I thought we should have been tipped into one of the canals, as we turned a sharp corner. Our men upset the baskets and stalls that encroached on the road, in the most unceremonious manner; but their proprietors did not seem to mind, many of them quietly moving their wares out of the way as they heard the shouts that announced our approach. The smell in the fish market was disgusting, and enough to poison the air for miles around, but the people did not seem to mind it in the least.

At last we left the river and town and, climbing a slight eminence, crossed the first moat by a stone bridge, and reached the guard house on the other side. There was some hesitation at first about admitting us; but it was soon overcome. Osaka castle, the last stronghold of the *shōgun*, is built on exactly the same plan as the castle we had already visited, but much stronger, being composed of enormous blocks of stone. One wonders how human labour could ever have transported them from their quarry to this place, for some measured forty feet long by twenty feet high.

We crossed the three moats and the three enclosures, now all full of barracks and soldiers. In the very centre, the old well and a little square tower are still standing, part of the *shōgun*'s original residence, which was destroyed by fire. The view from the top over the town and surrounding country is very fine. You can see countless streams coming from the mountains, and flowing into O River, on which Osaka is situated. The course of the river itself could be traced to the bay. And the line of coast to Kobe, and the far-off mountains in the Inland Sea were plainly visible.

On returning to the Mint we found luncheon awaiting us, and afterwards spent a pleasant time looking at a wonderful collection of curios.

The Imperial Mint of Japan is a large handsome building, in great force just now, for all of the old money is being called in and replaced. The contrast between the two moneys is very great. The ancient coinage consisted of long thin oval *ōban* and *koban*, worth from two dollars to eighteen pounds each, square silver *ichibugin*, and square copper pieces, with a hole in the centre. That which is taking its place is similar to European coinage, and is marked in English characters, and ornamented with Japanese devices, such as the phoenix and the dragon. It did not seem worthwhile to go minutely over the Mint, as it is arranged on exactly the same principle as the one in London, and the processes are carried out in the same manner.

Osaka used to be the emporium of all the inland commerce, and was considered the pearl of Japanese cities. After the revolution, and when the Mint was built, there was some intention of making it the capital of the empire. That idea was, however, abandoned; and the inconvenience of having the Mint so far away from the seat of government is greatly felt, all the bullion having to be sent backwards and forwards at great expense by sea. Commerce has now almost deserted Osaka, owing to the difficulty experienced by large ships in anchoring near the town, and the impossibility of their crossing the bar. The foreign consuls and representatives have all left the place for the newly established settlement at Kobe, where they feel safer, with men-of-war at anchor just under their windows.

There was just time to go round some of the old streets, and to some of the shops, before the hour by which we were due at the station. Osaka is famous for its waxworks and theatres. Five of the best of these have been burnt down within the last eighteen months, with terrible loss of life. We heard that a short time ago there was nearly serious trouble, in consequence of one of the managers having produced on the stage, in a most objectionable manner, a representation of the cruel and unprovoked assassination of an officer and two men, part of a boat's crew of a French ship. The English and French consuls went to the governor of the town, who promised that the piece should be stopped, and the obnoxious placards announcing the performance removed at once. But his instructions were not complied with, for the next day the piece was again performed, and the placards were still there. Some French sailors, luckily accompanied by their officers, saw the latter and wanted to tear them down, but they were persuaded to wait while the consuls were telegraphed for. They came at once, and again saw the governor, who sent some soldiers to stop the play and remove the bills; and so the affair ended peaceably.

We reached Kobe about seven o'clock, and went on board at once to dinner.

Arima

Saturday, February 10th

We were to have gone early this morning to Arima, a village in the mountains, situated among groves of bamboos, where there are mineral springs and an *onsen*, in which people bathe in the old style. But the weather was impossibly bad for our intended expedition, with showers of snow and sleet. We waited till half-past eleven, and then landed and talked of going to Osaka again by train, but finally decided that even this was not practicable, and that we had better stay and potter about at Kobe and Hyōgo.

The children set out to buy toys, whilst I went with a lady to pay another visit to the white horse and monkeys at the temple, and then walked on to a waterfall, prettily situated in a ravine, a little way behind the town. We afterwards visited several pawnbrokers' shops, at all of which there was something interesting to be seen. Many are perfect museums, but their proprietors never seem to care much to show you what they have, unless you are accompanied by a resident or someone they know. Then they invite you into the iron fire-proof 'godown' or store, at the back, and out of funny little boxes and bags and parcels produce all sorts of rare and curious things which have been sent to them to be sold, or which they may possibly have bought themselves. It is not of the slightest use to go to the large shops, full of things, if you want anything really good, for you will only find articles specially prepared for the European and American market.

I am very glad to hear that Dr. Charles Dresser is here, collecting, lecturing, and trying to persuade the Japanese to adhere to their own forms and taste in art and decoration. It is a great pity to observe the decadence of native art, and at the same time to see how much better the old things are than the new. A true Japanese artist never repeats himself, and consequently never makes an exact pair of anything. His designs agree generally, and his vases are more or less alike, without being a precise match. He throws in a spray of flowers, a bird, or a fan, as the fancy strikes him, and the same objects are therefore never placed in exactly the same relative position. Modern articles are made precisely alike, not only in pairs, but by the dozen and the hundred.

There are beautiful bantams to be seen in some of the shops here, but they cannot be bought, as they are private pets. They seem generally very small, and one I saw today had his head far behind his tail, which divided in the middle outwards, and fell forward on either side of his neck in the most extraordinary way. How he picked up his food and got through life, I am sure I don't know. There are plenty of little Japanese dogs; but they are not seen to advantage this cold weather, and there would be great difficulty in getting them home.

I bought some fine bantams at Yokohama, and a whole cage full of rice birds. They are the dearest little things, and spend most of the day bathing and twittering, occasionally getting all together into one nest, with their twenty-five heads peeping out. They are exactly like a magnified grain of rice, with legs and a bill. I hope I shall take them home alive, as they have borne the cold very well so far. We have also some mandarin ducks on board, and some gold and silver fish with two tails. Our sailors have over a hundred birds of their own, which never appear on deck, except on very sunny days. I don't know where they can keep them, unless they stow them away in their Japanese cabinets.

We went on board about dark, and a few friends came to dinner.

Sunday, February 11th
About 7 a.m., two Japanese officers came on board with a message nobody could understand. When we went on deck, we saw that all

the ships were dressed, and concluded that we had been asked to do the same; but we thought it better to send ashore to ascertain positively. The next difficulty was to get a Japanese flag. Thomas went on board the *Thabor*, a Japanese ship, to borrow one, and found everything was in bustle and confusion, news having arrived from Kyushu that the rebels were mustering in great force, and that they had seized some ships. The *Thabor*, *Mihu-maru*, and three others, are therefore to go through the Inland Sea to Nagasaki this afternoon.

The Japanese admiral sent word early this morning that he would come on board at two o'clock with some of his captains, and the French admiral also expressed a hope that it would be convenient to receive him and his captains at three. Their visits occupied nearly all the afternoon. We afterwards landed with the French admiral, paid some farewell visits, and went to look at a collection of old lacquer and Satsuma china, before we returned to the *Sunbeam*.

Prolonged Stay

Dipped in the lines of sunset, wreathed in zones,
The clouds are resting on their mountain thrones;
One peak alone exalts its glacier crest,
A golden paradise above the rest.
Thither the day with lingering steps retires,
And in its own blue element expires.

Monday, February 12th
Fires were lighted at 4 a.m., and by six we were steaming slowly out of the beautiful bay of Kobe. It was a cold bright morning, with a strong head wind, increasing every moment as we proceeded, until, in the Straits of Akashi, it became almost impossible to make any headway against it. There was not much sea, but the wind impeded our progress so much, that it was at last reduced to one mile instead of nine an hour. The straits are very fine, and the old castle presents an admirable specimen of the architecture of a *daimyō*'s residence.

We proceeded across the Harima Nada, where we were more or less exposed to the open sea, and where we took more water on board than we had done in the gale before arriving at Yokohama. There were no big waves, but we rolled tremendously, and the spray came over us, though the mere force of the wind seemed to keep the sea down.

After struggling until twelve o'clock, and having done but little good for the last three hours, Thomas determined to run back, and in a short time we found ourselves once more at anchor in the harbour of Kobe. It was a work of considerable difficulty, owing to the strong wind and tide, to steer safely among the numerous vessels, and for a few minutes we thought we were aground, as we did not make the slightest progress, though the engines were working ahead full speed. The provedore's boat came out to us as soon as we were seen, and we landed in her; but it was as much as the six stout oarsmen could do to make way against the wind.

We went for a walk, or rather a scramble, to the waterfall, halfway up to the Mayazan Tenjō-ji, or the Temple of the Moon, on Mount Maya. Much of the ground was covered with snow, the streams were frozen at the sides, and there were hanging icicles to be seen, six feet in length. And yet on either side were camellias and tea trees covered with red and white blossoms, orange trees, laden with fruit; goldfish swimming about in ponds, overhung with maidenhair fern, besides pteris and hothouse ferns, shaded by bamboos, palms, and castoroil plants. The order of vegetation seems to be as much reversed as everything else in this strange country. In England all those plants would require conservatories, or at least sheltered spots, and the greatest care, instead of being exposed to frost and snow.

Getting on board again was even a more difficult business than landing had been, but we arrived at last without mishap.

Tuesday, February 13th
The wind dropped at sunset, and as it continued calm all night, Thomas ordered fires to be lighted at 4 a.m. By six o'clock, however, it was blowing harder than ever, and we therefore decided to make an excursion to Arima instead of attempting another start.

We went ashore to make the necessary arrangements, and it was settled that we should start at ten o'clock, which we did, with the consulate constable as our guide.

We had three men to each *jinrikisha*, and went along at a merry pace through the long straggling towns of Kobe and Hyōgo. The cold was intense, and before we started our poor *jinrikisha* men were shivering until they nearly shook us out of the vehicles. Soon they were streaming with perspiration, and at our first halting-place they took off almost all their garments, though it was as much as we could do to keep warm in our furs and wraps. We waited while they partook copiously of hot tea and bowls of rice, and bought new straw shoes, or rather sandals, for less than a farthing a pair.

Today being the Japanese New Year's Day, all the little shrines in the houses and along the road were prettily decorated, and had offerings of rice, *sake*, and fruit deposited upon them. The spirits of the departed are supposed to come down and partake, not of the things themselves, but of the subtle invisible essence that rises from them. The road now became very pretty, winding through the valleys, climbing up and dipping down the various hills, and passing through picturesque villages, where all the people, leaving their meals or their games, came out to look at us, while some of the children scampered on to secure a good view of the foreigners, and others ran away frightened and screaming. They were all dressed in dark blue clothes, turned up with red, with bright embroidered *obi* and flowers in their elaborately dressed hair. I have managed to get some dolls' wigs, which give a good idea of the various styles of hair-dressing.

In rather more than three hours we reached Arima, a village far more beautifully situated than any we had seen, in the very centre of the mountains, where a dozen valleys converge into one centre. On one side are mineral springs, on the other a river. Bamboos grow luxuriantly on all sides, and the inhabitants of the various valleys obtain their livelihood by manufacturing from them all sorts of articles: boxes for every conceivable purpose; baskets, fine and coarse, large and small, useful and ornamental, coloured and plain; brushes, pipes, battledores and shuttlecocks, sticks, spoons, knives and forks, sauce ladles, boats, lamps, cradles, etc.

The first glimpse of the village is lovely; that from the bridge that crosses the river is still more so. We clambered up narrow streets, with quaint carved houses and overhanging balconies, till we reached a teahouse, kept by a closely shaven bonze, or priest. He seemed very pleased to see us, and bowed and shook hands over and over again. He placed his whole house at our disposal, and a very clean, pretty, and well-arranged house it was, with a lovely little formal garden, ornamented with mimic temples and bridges of ice, fashioned by the hard frost, with but little assistance from the hand of man. Bits of wood and stone, a few graceful fern-leaves and sprays of bamboo, and a trickling stream of water produced the most fairy-like crystalline effects imaginable. If only some good fairy could, with a touch of her wand, preserve it all intact until a few months hence, what a delight it would be in the hot summer weather!

Today the paper house was indeed cold, but even so slight a shelter from the bitter wind was acceptable, though we regretted the screens could not be opened to enable us to admire the prospect on all sides. The luncheon basket being quickly unpacked, the good priest warmed our food and produced a bottle of port wine, which he mulled for our benefit. Cheered and refreshed we proceeded on our way, leaving him much delighted with what seemed to us but a small recompense for his courtesy.

Every house and shop in those narrow picturesque streets was a study in itself, and so were the quaint groups of people we met, and who gazed eagerly at us. We looked into the public baths, two oblong tanks, into which the mineral springs came bubbling up, thick and yellow, and strongly impregnated with iron, at a temperature of 112°. They are covered in, and there is a rough passage round them. Here, in the bathing season, people of both sexes stand in rows, packed as tight as herrings in a barrel, and there are just as many outside waiting their turn to enter. Today there were only two bathers, immersed up to their chins in the steaming water. They had left all their clothes at home, and would shortly have to pass through the streets without any covering, notwithstanding the cold.

From the baths we went to some of the best basket shops, where the beauty and cheapness of the articles exposed for sale offered great temptations. We had to disturb our *jinrikisha* men, who were enjoying their frugal meal at a separate teahouse. It was beautifully served, and as clean and nicely cooked as possible, though consisting of viands which we might not have fancied, such as various kinds of fish, seaweed, sea snails (*bêche de mer*), and rice. Each man had his own little table and eight or ten separate dishes, a bottle of *sake*, tea pipe, and *hibachi*, arranged exactly as ours had been at the teahouse at Yokohama. How well they managed their chopsticks, how quickly they shovelled the food down, and how clean they left each dish! Habit is everything.

We were anxious to make the best of our way home, and starting at four, with but a short stop at the halfway teahouse, we reached the hotel soon after seven, having taken less than an hour to come five miles over a very bad road, an inch deep in mud. So much for a 'man-power carriage,' the literal translation of the word *jinrikisha*. Soon after an excellent dinner we returned on board, so as to be ready for an early start tomorrow morning.

Wednesday, February 14th

We were called at 4 a.m. Fires were lighted, but before steam was up the wind had risen; so our start was once more postponed to the afternoon. We steamed out to the buoy, from among the shipping, in order to be able to get away more easily at night. The wind generally goes down at sunset, and Tom hoped that, by taking our departure then, we should get through the worst part of the Inland Sea before the wind again rose with the sun.

After breakfast we went ashore, and dispersed in different directions, to meet again at the hotel for luncheon. Then we all again separated, the children going to the circus, whilst I took a drive, with a pair of black and white Hakodate ponies, to the foot of the hills behind the town.

It was a pleasant circuit by pretty valleys, and brought us back to the town by a different road. I went to pick up the children at the circus, and found them just coming out, with delighted faces, having most thoroughly enjoyed themselves. They went on board to tea, but Mabelle and I went with the consul in *jinrikisha* to a Japanese theatre at Hyōgo. The streets were crowded with holiday-makers; for today is the first of the Chinese new year, as yesterday was the first of the Japanese New Year. The floor of the theatre was crowded with people, all squatting on their heels, each with his or her chow-chow box and *hibachi* or brazier of burning charcoal to keep themselves warm. The performance frequently goes on for ten or twelve hours, with short intervals and whole families come and take up their abode at the theatre for twelve hours at a time. The acting was not at all bad, and the performers were beautifully dressed.

We did not stay very long at the theatre, but were soon tearing back again through the streets to the consulate. These quick rides in a *jinrikisha*, especially at night, are very amusing. You have the pleasure of going at a high speed, and yet, being on a level with the people, you can see much more of them and of their manners than would be possible in a carriage.

When we reached the consulate we found the chief of police of the foreign settlement waiting for the consul, to inform him that Japanese soldiers were patrolling the town with fixed bayonets, alleging that information had been sent to the governor that some of the rebels were in the hills at the back of the town, and might appear at any moment. The ships-of-war were to be communicated with at once for the protection of the inhabitants. They do not expect a general attack here, but seem to think the rebels' plan is to creep up by degrees to Osaka, where the emperor is shortly expected to stay, and take possession of his person and the imperial treasure at one blow.

When I got on board the *Sunbeam* again, I found that steam was up and all was ready for starting; but the wind was still strong against us, and it was evidently necessary again to wait until four o'clock to-morrow morning.

We were rolling a good deal, and, coming along the engine-room passage, my foot slipped, a door banged to, and my thumb was caught in the hinge and terribly crushed. Dressing it was a very painful affair, as the doctor had to ascertain whether the bone was broken, and I fainted during the operation. At last I was carried to my cabin and put to bed, after taking a strong dose of chloral to soothe the agonising pain.

Fire!

Thursday, February 15th

I wonder if anybody who has not experienced it can realise the stupefying, helpless sensation of being roused up from a sound sleep, in the middle of the night, on board ship, by the cry of 'Fire!' and finding oneself enveloped in a smoke so dense as to render everything invisible.

At 2.30 a.m. I was awakened by a great noise and a loud cry of 'The ship is on fire!' followed by Mr. Bingham rushing into our cabin to wake us. At first I could hardly realise where we were, or what was happening, as I was half stupid with chloral, pain, and smoke, which was issuing from each side of the staircase in dense volumes. My first thought was for the children, but I found they had not been forgotten. Rolled up in blankets, they were already in transit to the deck-house. In the meantime Mr. Bingham had drenched the flames with every available jug of water, and Thomas had roused the crew, and made them screw the hose on to the pump. They were afraid to open the hatches, to discover where the fire was, until the hose and extinguishers were ready to work, as they did not know whether or not the hold was on fire, and the whole ship might burst into a blaze the moment the air was admitted. Allen soon appeared with an extinguisher on his back, and the mate with the hose. Then the cupboard in Mr. Bingham's room was opened, and burning cloaks, dresses, boxes of curios, portmanteaus, etc., were hauled out, and, by a chain of men, sent on deck, where they were drenched with seawater or thrown overboard. Moving these things caused the flames to increase in vigour, and the extingguisher was used freely, and with the greatest success. It is an invaluable invention, especially for a yacht, where there are so many holes and corners that it would be impossible to reach by ordinary means. All this time the smoke was pouring in volumes from the cupboard on the other side, and from under the nursery fireplace. The floors were pulled up, and the partitions were pulled down, until at last the flames were got under. The holds were next examined. No damage had been done there; but the cabin floor was completely burnt through, and the lead from the nursery fireplace was running about, melted by the heat.

The explanation of the cause of the fire is very simple. Being a bitterly cold night, a roaring fire had been made up in the nursery, but about half-past ten the servants thought it looked rather dangerous and raked it out. The ashpan was not large enough, however, to hold the hot embers, which soon made the tiles red-hot. The woodwork caught fire, and had been smouldering for hours, when the nurse fortunately woke and discovered the state of affairs. She tried to rouse the other maids, but they were stupefied with the smoke, and so she rushed off at once to the doctor and Mr. Bingham. The former seized a child under each arm, wrapped them in blankets, and carried them off to the deck-house, Mabelle and the maids following, with more blankets and rugs, hastily snatched up. The children were as good as possible. They never cried nor made the least fuss, but composed themselves in the deck-house to sleep for the remainder of the night, as if it were all a matter of course. When I went to see them, little Muriel [Brassey] remarked: 'If the yacht is on fire, mamma, had not baby and I better get our ulsters, and go with Emma in the boat to the hotel, to be out of the way?' It is the third time in their short lives that they have been picked out of bed in the middle of the night and carried off in blankets away from a fire, so I suppose they are getting quite used to it.

There can be no doubt that the preservation of the *Sunbeam* from very serious damage, if not from complete destruction, was due to the prompt and efficient manner in which the extinguishers were used. It was not our first experience of the value of this invention; for, not very long before we undertook our present expedition, a fire broke out in our house in London, on which occasion the extinguishers we fortunately had at hand rendered most excellent service in subduing the flames.

By half-past three all danger was past, and we began to settle down again, though it took a long time to get rid of the smoke.

Inland Sea

At four o'clock we weighed anchor, and once more made a start from Kobe, and passed through the Straits of Akashi. The wind was dead ahead, but not so strong as when we made our previous attempts. It was bitterly cold, the thermometer, in a sheltered place, being only one degree above freezing, and the breeze from the snowy mountains cutting like a knife.

We were all disappointed with our sail today; perhaps because we had heard so much of the extreme beauty of the scenery, and this is not the best time of year for seeing it. The hills are all brown, instead of being covered with luxuriant vegetation, and all looked bleak and barren, though the outlines of the mountain ranges were very fine. We were reminded of the west coast of Scotland, the Lofoten Islands in the Arctic Circle, and the tamer portions of the scenery of the Straits of Magellan.

After passing through the Straits, we crossed the Harima Nada— rather a wider portion of the sea—and then entered the intricate channels among the islands once more. There are three thousand of them altogether, so one may take it for granted that the navigation is by no means easy. The currents and tides are strong, sunken rocks are frequent, and the greatest care is required. Indeed, many people at Yokohama urged Thomas to take a pilot.

We had one lovely view in the afternoon of the Shōdo Island, with its snowy mountain at the back, and a pretty little village, with a few picturesque junks in the foreground. The *Sunbeam* passed between Ogi-jima and Te-shima, steering straight for the cone-shaped little island of Ozuchi.

Towards dusk we made the Nabe-shima lighthouse off Yo-shima, and, steering past it, had to take several sharp and awkward turns, to avoid two reefs off Hon-jima and Ushi-shima. Thus we threaded the Shiaku Seto strait, and, avoiding the Oki no Su bank by another sharp turn, dropped anchor at Marugame, on the southern side of Hiroshima Island, precisely at 8.30 p.m. Thomas had been on the lookout since 5 a.m., and we were all more or less worn out with the fatigue and excitement of last night.

Friday, February 16th
Off again at 4 a.m. The scenery was much finer than yesterday, and the wind not quite so bitterly cold.

About 11 a.m. I heard a hurrying to and fro, and once more the cry of 'Fire!' This time it was in the store-room that it broke out. The iron plates on which the saloon and galley grates are fixed had become red-hot, and the wooden deck below had consequently caught fire. The boxes on both sides, containing the stores, were in flames; but they were quickly removed, water was poured down, and the second and third fires were thus soon extinguished.

Shimonoseki

Saturday, February 17th

At 3.15 a.m. we began to slow; at 3.45 the anchor was dropped near the lighthouse of Hesaki, and we waited until daylight before proceeding through the Straits of Shimonoseki. About nine o'clock a fresh start was made, under steam, but before long the wind freshened, and as soon as the anchorage near the town was reached we let go once more, near two men-of-war, who had preceded us from Kobe, but who were now wind-bound, like ourselves.

To our astonishment, we also saw a large ship from Nova Scotia at anchor, the *Mary Fraser* although this is not a free port, nor within treaty limits. The gig was lowered at once, and we rowed alongside to gain what intelligence could be learned, as well as to ascertain what likelihood there might be of our obtaining fresh supplies here. The captain was very civil and kind, and volunteered to go on shore with us and act as our interpreter.

We landed opposite a large teahouse, where we were immediately surrounded by a crowd of Japanese, who stared at us eagerly and even touched us, only through curiosity. They pursued us wherever we went, and when we entered a teahouse or shop the whole crowd immediately stopped, and if we retired to the back they surged all over the front premises, and penetrated into the interior as far as they could.

A most amusing scene took place at one of the teahouses, where we went to order some provisions for the *Sunbeam*. It was rather a tedious process, and when we came out of the back room we found the whole of the front of the place filled by a gaping, curious crowd. The proprietor suggested that they should retire at once, and an abrupt retreat immediately took place, the difficulties of which were greatly augmented by the fact that everyone had left his high wooden shoes outside, along the front of the house. The street was ankle deep in mud and half-melted snow, into which they did not like to venture in their stockings; but how the owners of two or three hundred pairs of clogs, almost exactly alike, ever found their own property again I do not understand, though they managed to clear out very quickly. I believe Muriel and I were the chief objects of attraction. They told us that no European lady or child had ever been at Shimonoseki before. It is not a treaty port, so no one is allowed to land, except from a man-of-war, without special permission, which is not often given. It is, besides, the key to the Inland Sea, and the authorities are very jealous about any one seeing the forts. There is only one European resident here, connected with the telegraph, and a dull time he must have of it. The wire crosses the Straits a few miles higher up.

The streets appeared to be full of soldiers, patrolling singly and in pairs, with fixed bayonets. The temples were being used as barracks, and the principal buildings seemed to be strongly guarded, but otherwise everything appeared to go on as usual.

We waded through the mud and snow to the proverbial end of all things, always followed by the same crowd, and stared at by all the inhabitants of the houses we passed. They seemed very timid, and inclined to run away as soon as we turned round. Still, their curiosity, especially respecting my sealskin jacket and serge dress, was insatiable, and I constantly felt myself being gently stroked and touched.

We returned to the *Sunbeam*, and whilst we were at lunch some officers came on board to say that, this not being a treaty port, we could not purchase any provisions, except through them, and with special permission. This was soon arranged, and our visitors were rewarded for their trouble by being shown over the yacht.

Sunday, February 18th

We were awakened in the night by a heavy gale, with snow and sleet beating furiously on the deck. In the morning the land was covered with snow, the water froze as it was pumped on deck, and the bitter wind howled and whistled through the rigging. In the afternoon the wind even increased in violence, the snowstorms became more frequent, and the sky was dark and overcast.

We had service at eleven and again at four. The sun set cold and stormy, promising a wild night. At times the shore was quite hidden by the snowstorms, though only a few cables' lengths off.

Departure

Monday, February 19th

The wind and weather became worse than ever, and, as time was precious, Thomas decided to retrace our steps for a short distance and go through the Bungo Straits, between the islands of Shikoku and Kyushu, instead of going out to sea through the Shimonoseki Straits, as, in the latter case, the gale would be right in our teeth, and we should make but little progress. Now we shall be under the shelter of Kyushu and the Ōsumi and Ryūkyū Islands for at least two days, and so make a fair wind of it. Steering due south, too, we may hope to be soon out of this horrid weather. The only drawback to this plan is that we shall miss seeing Nagasaki, which I much regret. There are no great sights there, but the scenery is pretty, and the place is interesting owing to the fact that it was the first and for many years the only, port open to foreigners, and also the scene of the cruel murders of Christians and the site of the beautiful island of Takoboko. Shanghai I do not think I regret so much, though Thomas would have been interested to talk with the merchants about their commerce, and to see their houses, many of which are, I am told, perfect palaces. It would be very cold there, too, at this time of year; and I do so long to lose my cough and feel warm once more.

At 8.30 p.m. we weighed and proceeded under steam. The views of the mountains, between the snowstorms, were lovely, with the fresh-fallen snow shining in an occasional gleam of sunshine. We soon passed the Hesaki light, with wind and tide in our favour, and at sunset found ourselves in the open waters of the North Pacific.

Glossary

bonsai:	Art form using cultivation techniques to produce small trees that mimic the shape and scale of full size trees.
daimyō:	Feudal lord.
geisha:	A woman professionally trained to entertain customers with music, dancing, food and drinks, and witty stories.
gohei:	Wooden wands, decorated with two *shide* (zigzagging paper streamers) used in Shinto rituals.harakiri: The act of disembowelment.
hibachi:	Small Japanese charcoal heating appliance somewhat resembling a brazier.
ichibugin:	Square silver plate Tokugawa currency. One ôban was equivalent to a quarter ryô.kago: Palanquin.
koban:	Oval gold plate Tokugawa currency. One ôban was equivalent to one ryō.
ōban:	Monetary oval gold plate Tokugawa currency. One *ōban* was equivalent to ten *ryō*, or ten *koban*, with a weight of 165 g.
obi:	Broad sash for a *kimono*.
onsen:	Hot spring.
jinrikisha:	Rickshaw.

sake:	Japanese rice wine.
shōgun:	Hereditary military ruler during Japan's feudal era.
shōji:	Lightweight sliding doors covered with paper.
tokonoma:	Alcove.
urushi:	Japanese lacquerware, lacquered with the resin of the urushi tree.
yashiki:	Samurai mansion.

TOYO PRess: Explore Dream Discover
Editorial supervision: William de Lange. Book and
cover design: Chōkei Studios. Printing and binding:
IngramSpark. The typeface used is Linux Biolinum O.